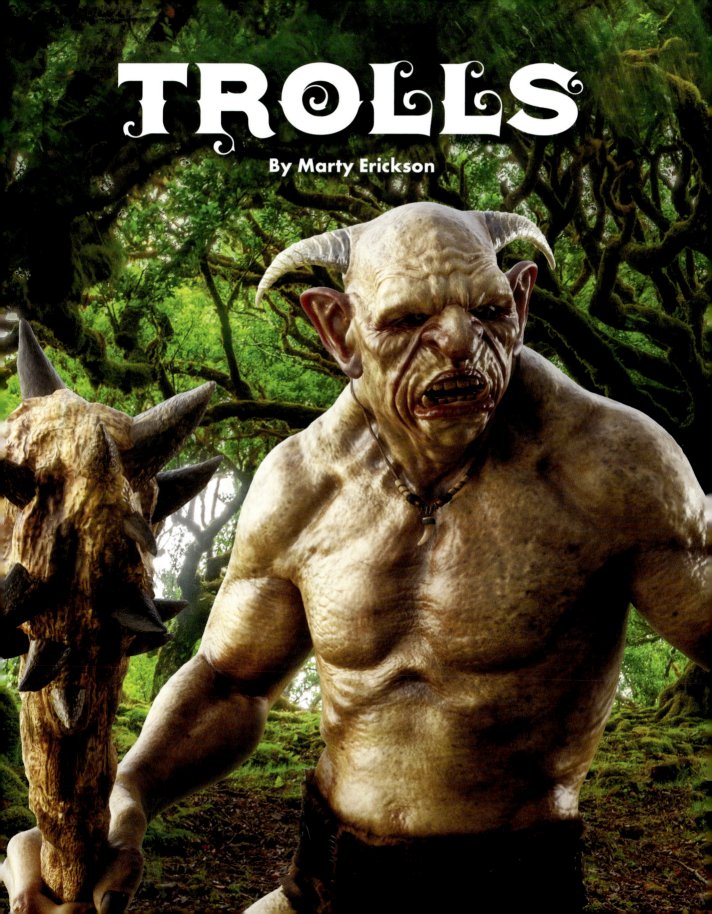

Published by The Child's World®
1980 Lookout Drive • Mankato, MN 56003-1705
800-599-READ • www.childsworld.com

Photographs ©: Shutterstock Images, cover (troll), 1 (troll), 10–11, 13, 19, 21; Piotr Krzeslak/Shutterstock Images, cover (background) 1–3 (background); Tracy K. P. Gregg, 5; iStockphoto, 6, 9, 15; Ken Schulze/Shutterstock Images, 14; Dave Logan/iStockphoto, 16; Steve Lagreca/Shutterstock Images, 18, 23; Ju See/Shutterstock Images, 20, 24

Copyright © 2022 by The Child's World®
All rights reserved. No part of this book may be reproduced or utilized in any form or by any means without written permission from the publisher.

ISBN 9781503849808 (Reinforced Library Binding)
ISBN 9781503850828 (Portable Document Format)
ISBN 9781503851580 (Online Multi-user eBook)
LCCN 2021939671

Printed in the United States of America

Table of Contents

CHAPTER ONE

Troll Wars...4

CHAPTER TWO

History of Trolls...8

CHAPTER THREE

Staying Hidden...12

CHAPTER FOUR

Trolls Today...18

Glossary...22

To Learn More...23

Index...24

CHAPTER ONE

TROLL WARS

Miguel and his mom visited Iceland. There were many legends about trolls there, and Miguel loved learning about them. Miguel and his mom went on a hike. In the middle of a green field, huge dark rocks seemed to sprout from the ground.

The rocks looked like dark **pillars**. Some were taller than Miguel's mom. Miguel stood next to a pillar. It was much taller than he was. Two people from Iceland passed them. They told Miguel and his mom about a legend. More than 1,000 years ago, trolls fought a war against one another. They threw these rocks. The pillars were all that was left from the troll wars.

Lava pillars are common in the ocean. But it is rare to see them on land. Researchers study the lava pillars to learn more about them.

Trolls in Iceland are sometimes called huldufólk, or "hidden folk."

Miguel loved the story. But he knew it was not true. Miguel and his mom looked for answers. The pillars actually formed from lava flows. The lava pushed up through the ground. It made the unique forms. Still, Miguel loved to think trolls may have lived in Iceland at one time.

Trolls are legendary creatures. Most stories about them come from northern Europe. Some stories describe trolls as dangerous. Others describe them as friendly.

Over time, stories about trolls changed. But one thing has not changed. People continue to make up new stories about trolls. Movies and books about trolls capture people's imaginations.

CHAPTER TWO

HISTORY OF TROLLS

Legends of trolls exist in many different northern European cultures. One example is in Norse **mythology**. Norse mythology came from Vikings. Vikings lived in countries that are now Sweden, Norway, and Denmark. They lived between approximately 800 and 1000 AD.

Storytellers passed legends down **orally**. People told stories of trolls and other mythical creatures. The stories changed slightly with each retelling. They described many creatures that people now think of as trolls.

Vikings passed down stories orally rather than by writing them down. Each time a story was told, it changed a little bit.

Lightning is one of the only things that scares trolls.

People from Iceland wrote down these stories for the first time in the 1200s. That way, stories could be read for years to come. The collection is called the *Edda*. The *Edda* has many different stories from Iceland. People can still read the *Edda* today.

Folklore from **Scandinavia** described different kinds of trolls. Some were large and frightening.

They ate and attacked people. Others were small. No matter their size, trolls did not like humans. Trolls in these stories were said to be scared of church bells. They were also scared of lightning. This is because Thor, the Norse god of thunder, hunted trolls.

CHAPTER THREE
STAYING HIDDEN

Often, descriptions of trolls change depending on the story. But trolls have some things in common. They walk on two legs. Some stories say trolls have hunched backs. They have humanlike features. Some trolls are more humanlike than others. Many drawings of trolls show them with large noses.

Some stories say different kinds of trolls live in different areas. There are mountain, forest, and cave trolls. Descriptions of trolls are different in different stories. But legends say a troll blends in with its **habitat**. Mountain and cave trolls have brown or gray skin. This helps them blend in with rocks.

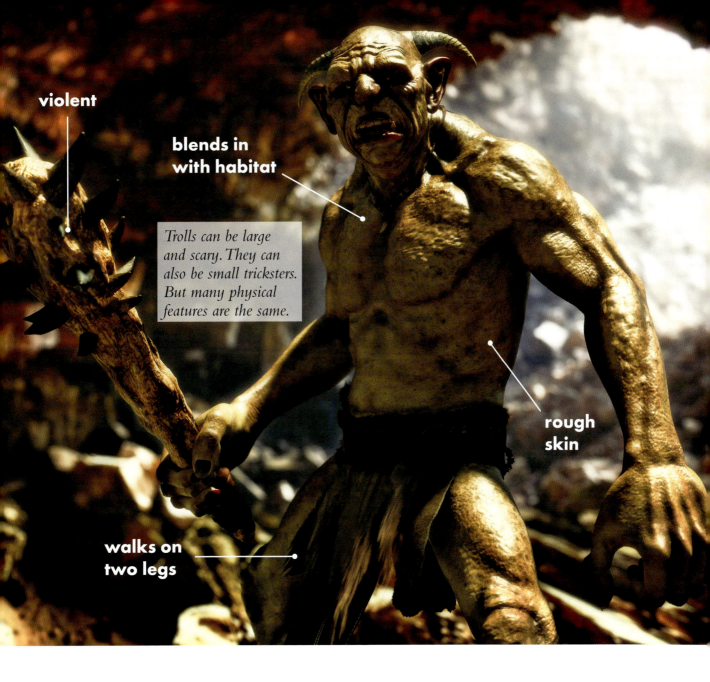

violent

blends in with habitat

Trolls can be large and scary. They can also be small tricksters. But many physical features are the same.

rough skin

walks on two legs

Stories say forest trolls make clothes for themselves. They put moss, leaves, and other plants on their bodies. Their skin is greenish brown or gray.

In some stories, trolls throw stones at people to protect their land.

Many stories of trolls describe them as fearsome. Images show trolls with sharp teeth. They have strong muscles. Large trolls can uproot a tree. They can throw huge stones. Some stories blame trolls for destroyed churches. Other stories say trolls eat people.

Other troll stories say the creatures are small. Some are kind and helpful toward humans. Others are **mischievous**. They try to trick humans. They tell riddles that humans must solve. Some stories say small trolls can make humans see things that aren't there. Trolls can make humans lose track of time or fall asleep.

Small trolls can be friendly or mischievous.

In many stories, trolls live under bridges and demand payment from travelers.

Legends say trolls are protective of their lands. Stories from Scandinavia say trolls kidnap people. Trolls might also take over or destroy farms that are too close to the trolls' homes. In some stories, trolls throw huge boulders at passing travelers.

Many popular stories tell of trolls living under bridges. A troll might make people pay money to cross the bridge. If a person cannot pay, stories say the troll may hurt the person. Or it may scare the person away.

CHAPTER FOUR

TROLLS TODAY

Trolls do not exist in real life. But they still inspire awe. People name landmarks after trolls. For example, Troll Tongue is in Norway. It is a large rock that sticks out from a mountain. It looks like a troll's tongue. People visit Norway to see the landmark.

People also create art inspired by trolls. **Sculptures** of trolls exist around the world. A statue of a troll lives under a bridge in Seattle, Washington. It is 18 feet (5.5 m) tall.

The Fremont Troll in Seattle was designed by Steve Badanes.

In Norwegian, Troll Tongue is called Trolltunga. *This landmark is in Odda, Norway.*

Trolls from the Trolls movies and toys have tall, colorful hair.

Trolls do not just exist in sculptures and landmarks. These creatures appear in movies, in books, and as toys. Each book, movie, or toy shows trolls a little differently.

The *Trolls* movies are based on a toy line. Trolls in these movies are small and sweet. They have brightly colored hair. In the *Harry Potter* books and movies, trolls are big. They are not very smart.

It is their size that makes them dangerous. Trolls in the *Frozen* movies have rough, gray skin. They use moss and leaves as clothes. These trolls are kind and helpful.

Stories of trolls are all a little different. Each story chooses to show trolls in unique ways. People will continue to make up new stories about trolls.

Scary trolls are part of the Lord of the Rings *movies.*

GLOSSARY

habitat (HAB-uh-tat) A habitat is the place where a creature normally lives. A troll's appearance changes depending on its habitat.

mischievous (MISS-chuv-vuhss) Someone who is mischievous behaves in an annoying or slightly harmful way. In some stories, small trolls are mischievous and try to trick humans.

mythology (mith-AH-loh-jee) Mythology is a collection of stories that are not true, but are believed or popular. Norse mythology includes stories of trolls.

orally (OR-uh-lee) To tell a story orally means to tell it out loud. Vikings passed stories down orally, so stories changed over time.

pillars (PILL-uhrs) Pillars are towers, often made of stone. In Iceland, a legend says pillars sticking up from the ground are all that is left from a troll war.

Scandinavia (scan-dih-NAY-vee-uh) Scandinavia refers to the countries of Norway, Sweden, and Denmark, and sometimes Finland and Iceland. Many legends from Scandinavia tell stories of trolls.

sculptures (SKUHLP-chuhrs) Sculptures are pieces of art formed out of rock, wood, or other materials. People make troll sculptures.

TO LEARN MORE

In the Library

Alexander, Heather. *A Child's Introduction to Norse Mythology.*
New York, NY: Black Dog & Leventhal, 2018.

Dillard, Sheri. *Viking Warriors.* Mankato, MN:
The Child's World, 2015.

Rowley, Kris Erickson, and Sara Cucini. *Trolls.* New York, NY:
AV2 by Weigl, 2020.

On the Web

Visit our website for links about trolls:

childsworld.com/links

Note to Parents, Teachers, and Librarians: We routinely verify our Web links to make sure they are safe and active sites. So encourage your readers to check them out!

INDEX

appearance, 10–11, 12–15, 20–21

behavior, 4–7, 11, 14–17, 20–21

bridges, 17, 18

Frozen, 21

Harry Potter, 20–21

Iceland, 4–7, 10

lava pillars, 4–7

riddles, 15

Thor, 11

Trolls, 20

Vikings, 8

ABOUT THE AUTHOR

Marty Erickson is a writer living in Minnesota. They write books for young people full time and like to go hiking.